Rediscovering
Our Heart

Experiencing Fulfillment

by Mahi

Rediscovering Our Heart
Experiencing Fulfillment
by Mahi
© United States 1999

Sunstar Publishing, Ltd.
204 S. 20th Street
Fairfield, Iowa 52556

First Edition 1999

Printed in the United States of America

Library of Congress Catalog Card Number: 98-060180

ISBN: 1-887472-51-7

Cover Design, Amanda Collett
Book Design, Irene Archer

The information in this book is meant to be a blessing. However, this information is not medical advice. Neither the author, nor any persons or organizations associated with the author, are in any way liable for others or any effects resulting from practicing this information.

Readers interested in obtaining further information on the subject matter of this book are invited to correspond with:

The Secretary, Sunstar Publishing, Ltd.
P.O. Box 2211, Fairfield, Iowa 52556
More Sunstar books at: http://www.newagepage.com

Much love,

Mahi

Other Books by Mahi

A Dream…Once Upon a Quiet Mind
A Medicine Called Love
Organizing for Fulfillment
Letters to my Lover

This book is dedicated to
Mom ♡

Thank you Patricia Florin, Denise Poole, Irene Archer, Amanda Collett, and Rodney Charles for your support in creating this book. Thank you Mom and Dad for bringing me to this place. Thank you, my dear Heart, for this life and love we are sharing. ❧

Contents

My love for you is total
complete
eternal.
Having forgotten the experience of this love
you doubt it now
even as the feeling of it wells up within you.
And you are faced with a choice
to call this feeling a lie
or to embrace it as truth.

Your next moment hinges on this decision.
Your life turns on this pivotal point.
Your next experience revolves on this perception
your Mind's perception
of what dwells within you.

Am I love?
Or am I fear?

All of us can speak to our Heart,
and the moment we do,
we begin to write our own story.

CHAPTER ONE

Heart

My Heart! Where are you?

I am here.

Sometimes I feel like I've lost you.

Do not worry. I am never lost.

But I am worried. Sometimes I don't feel anything, like I am Heartless. Other times I have so many feelings, but I don't know how to express them. I don't really understand myself. I try to figure it out, but I get confused.

When you get confused, listen to your Heart.

How do I do that?

By recognizing my voice. I speak through feeling. The feeling of love.

And what about all of these other feelings? Where do they come from?

You create them.

What do you mean, "I" create them? If you are my Heart, then who am "I"?

You are the Mind, the creator of experience. I am the Heart, the source of experience. I am not created. Nor am I ever destroyed. I am that which exists before any creation occurs. I am that which is present in the midst of any experience that the Mind conjures up. And I am that which remains after each experience has passed away.

The Heart is energy without form. The Mind is energy in the form of bodies of experience.

The Heart is unconditioned energy. The Mind is energy that has been conditioned.

The physical body is the actualization of the Mind. Through the Mind (in the form of body) it becomes possible to have an experience.

And what if I don't like my experience? What if I feel confused, or worried, or afraid?

Then listen to your Heart.

How do I do that? I know you've just explained. But there are so many feelings, so many voices, how can I trust which one is yours?

Remember this: There is only one original feeling— Love. This feeling is not created and hence it requires no thought, work, or effort to be felt. Love is my voice. This is my wisdom. All other feelings are created by the Mind.

Unconditional love is the only feeling that I send. My

energy, or emotion, has been given many words. Here I will define myself as the grandest feeling you have ever felt. I am a feeling of peace, joy, bliss, unity, harmony, wholeness, completeness, oneness.

And where does everything else come from? How does it all get started?

All things originate from me. I am the source. I am intrinsic feeling. I am non-created. I am pure energy. All else is imagined. Imagination is powerful, molding energy into form. Energy cannot be created, but it can be used to create with. Energy can be changed, shifted, shaped, and reshaped.

With the very first thought, the Mind came into being. With the birth of Mind, there was created the appearance of something other than myself. As soon as some of my energy took the form of something other than the whole, the relative world was born. At that point it became possible to have a relationship. By taking different forms, I am able to relate to myself. In this way it is possible to have an experience.

Whenever the Mind thinks a thought, it is making a sort of judgment. Each thought circles about in the Mind. Each judgment creates a boundary. Thoughts eventually manifest into the physical boundaries of the human body, as well as everything else in the Universe. Through your body you experience the effects of your thoughts or judgments. In each moment you feel the effects of your present state of Mind.

Some beings experience these boundaries and bodies as limiting. However, the limits (boundaries) of your Mind and body are precisely what free you to relate to others and thus experience your 'self.' Ultimately there are no 'others,' nor are there any limits. By allowing my self to be molded into beings of many forms, I am able to have relationships, experience myself overcoming limits, and move toward an expanding sense of joy and love.

The source of the universe is love. This unconditional energy of love can be used to mold an unlimited variety of experiences. The Mind directs the flow.

All experiences begin with either a thought of love or a thought of fear. The thought of love creates expansion and leaves the Mind open to the feeling of love from which it was formed. The thought of fear causes the Mind to close up and experience separation from the Heart.

Why do we become separate?

We don't. We have never been separate. The Mind cannot exist without the Heart. We are One. You are an extension of me. Your very existence depends upon your connection to me. You are made of my energy. You are flesh of my flesh, bone of my bone, blood of my blood.

The experience of separation is an illusion. All experiences (other than the feeling of love) originate from a thought. Feelings of loneliness or separation originate from a fearful thought or judgment. Fear is the sponsoring thought of all experiences that feel painful. The thought of fear is the sponsor of separation, loneliness, confusion, conflict, and suffering.

How do I get back in touch with you?

We must build a bridge between us, the Heart and Mind. In truth, the bridge is already there, in the form of Spirit. Through the feeling and communion of my Spirit, you are saved from the experience of eternal pain and separation. But you are not always sure how to recognize my voice.

'Nothing' is required to invoke my Spirit. I am felt in the quiet Mind. The Mind that is thoughtless is without judgment and it is from this state that you can sense my unconditional nature. Then you can begin to create consciously and powerfully, using me to form the conditions of your life. When we are communicating, you are able to consciously choose your path.

My path?

Yes, each individual being is creating a personal journey. The Mind is the tool for creating the journey and the body is the vehicle for experiencing (feeling) what you create.

Each moment you are using your present thoughts, language, circumstances, and body to experience your self. As we journey through life together, the Mind changes, and the body transforms.

Since everyone has a Heart, what do we need one another for?

You don't. No one needs anyone else. Not only do all beings have a Heart, but all of you are of one Heart. You originate from one, but you possess different states of Mind, which are reflected through different bodies (beings). When two or more individual beings remember their Heart, it becomes possible to share love and wisdom without fighting over the source.

By taking the form of different bodies, each with its own Mind and will, we have created an opportunity to share experience. Through your individuality you can create and share whatever experience you are able to imagine from your present state of being.

This opportunity is not an obligation. The sense of obligation is created when you imagine that you 'need' one another, hungrily viewing each 'other' as a source of survival. Forgetting your true source, you forget how to give and share from your Heart. Instead of feeling the freedom of love, you feel limited. You obligate yourself to one another and fear causes you to feel bound by that obligation.

When people fear one another, they create the illusion that energy, life, and love are lacking. Instead of creating and sharing together, people start to work for whoever controls the most energy. You attempt to 'earn' one another's favor. You fight and compete with one another for what appears to be limited.

The Mind that feels limited attempts to take from others. You justify this by thinking of others as 'evil.' You withhold love because you feel weak. You attempt to make others feel weaker than you. This creates conflict. For no being is willing to remain dependent upon another for the love that exists within themselves.

Controlling others by making them dependent upon you leads to resentment. Resentment is the inability to forgive or to let go of fearful judgments (thoughts).

Fear is a grasping for love. When you fear, you doubt that which already is. Grasping for life and love is a doubting of one's own Heart. This leads to death.

I reMind you that energy, life, and love are not lacking. They are abundant. Not only are they abundant, but they are eternal. I also reMind you that your Heart is not evil or limited. Quite the opposite. Nothing could be further from the truth than the thought that you are intrinsically evil. However, the Mind is powerful when it comes to creating experiences. The existence of evil began with the first thought (judgment) of yourself as evil. This idea places you in bondage. Rather than save you, it has led to many deaths.

I thought you said there was no death.

There isn't. But your body exists in the relative dimension of Mind, where energy responds to the thoughts you have about it. Your body is the product of generations of thought. When you believe the life of your energetic self to be 'limited,' your body responds by breaking down. Meanwhile, the energy of your self is never actually destroyed, but it does change form.

The experience of death is an illusion created by the fearful Mind. When a person becomes fully aware of their Heart and source of being, unconscious fear and death pass away.

As your awareness increases you may share your love …inspiring and empowering one another. You may choose to reMind one another of the abundance of love, of life, and of joy. No longer will you feel the need to compete and rob one another for that which all of you possess in abundant measure. Fear and its painful effects will end when you acknowledge your inner nature of love.

Is this journey going to be complicated?

Our journey together did not begin yesterday. Nor did it begin with this human life. We have always been together, experiencing different aspects of our self. The cycles of birth and death are just one aspect. Complexity is another.

The wisdom of the Heart is simple. The creations of the Mind are many, and hence that creates the appearance of complexity. However, no matter what the Mind creates or how complex these creations appear, the same underlying principle of creation is present.

All creation occurs through the same process, a process in which the Mind directs energy into form. The created forms exist in varying levels or dimensions of physicality that all relate and interact to make up the universe of infinite experiences.

When you become fully conscious of the creative process, it becomes possible to direct that process. You no longer need to be the victim of outward circumstances. Both pain and joy have the same underlying cause—you.

Remember, it is you who are directing the flow of life. The Mind is the cause, your body of experience is the effect. *Thoughts are cause, the way you feel is the effect.*

All of these words are coming from you as you ponder our relationship. I don't say anything. It is the Mind that thinks, speaks, and acts. I am simply your lover. My love is profound in its simplicity. My love is simple because it is unconditional.

I am the source of energy that allows you to carry on no matter how many times you stumble. I am the life within you that continues no matter how many deaths you create for yourself. If your life or philosophies are getting too complicated for you, then change them. I am only here to reMind you of your ability and potential to do that.

Are you saying that life does not have to be complicated?

Life need not be complex. Nor need it be a struggle. Life is intrinsically simple because it is eternal. In other words it requires no effort, work or maintenance. It is only a specific experience of life that requires maintenance or ongoing attention.

Creating a complex and struggling life requires a great deal of effort and continued maintenance. Complexities, suffering, and problems don't just happen. They require work. Problems and pain continue because you continue to give them attention …the attention (thoughts) of fear and worry.

Rather than using my unconditional love energy to play, dance, make music, and rejoice, you have directed it toward the struggle to survive. This struggle is a statement of doubt. You doubt life. And since you are the creator of your journey, you end up going through an illusionary experience of struggle and death. This doubt is motivated by fear. Fear is blind to love. Fear resists and denies the abundant energy that I eternally provide.

Is there another way?

You have the potential to create joy. Move toward that. You have an opportunity to experience love. Feel that.

It is difficult to feel love within the clamor of the worried Mind. A Mind that is attached to fear-based logic or philosophy is stuck in a struggle with itself, trying to earn the life and love which already IS and always has been.

You create destruction in your worried attempts to save yourself. The Mind holds on to fear-based philosophies for dear life, believing that life depends upon maintaining a firm grasp. The truth is that any thought, logic, or philosophy that is sponsored by fear destroys life, in the relative sense.

The logical Mind will not let go of fear unless given a reason. So I will provide reason. I will make clear the wisdom of love. But all of the explaining in the world will not substitute for personal experience. This is what you are doing here on earth, in your various bodily forms. You are gaining the personal experience that love is all there is. When this experience has occurred, explanations are no longer necessary.

How can I experience you more fully in my life?

Do not worry. You exist to be filled with my love. You are the body and boundary that contain me. You are 'bound' to be fulfilled.

The Heart is the beginning, the end, and the beginning again. There are many experiences, but they all come back to me. For the Mind is a circle, and I am its source.

Everything is a matter of Soul.

CHAPTER TWO

Soul

What do you mean when you say the Mind is a circle?

The Mind flows in circles, many circles, and I, the Heart, exist in the center. Together we form a sphere… the sphere of our Soul.

My Soul is a sphere?

Yes, a versatile, creative sphere. Our Soul has the power to change form and take many shapes, creating the reality you experience. Yet regardless of the experience, we remain as one.

The universe can be described in countless ways. Here is one explanation.

The universe is a Soul. The Soul has three aspects, consisting of Heart, Mind, and Spirit. These three parts of the Soul are simply three qualities of one being.

The Soul has the form or shape of a sphere. The center, or core of this sphere, is the Heart. The Heart is eternal. The Soul may contract or expand, but the core of the Soul, the Heart, remains the same. The Heart is motionless and spaceless, and therefore timeless.

Everything that emanates outward from the Heart is the Mind. The Mind is an extension of the Heart.

Spirit is the messenger, the communication network of the Soul. Spirit connects one part of the Soul to every other part. Spirit carries messages from the Heart to the Mind.

Every being is a Soul, and all beings exist within one Soul of the universe. The experience of individuality is created when the one Universal Soul creates pockets of awareness within the sphere of its self. Each individual being is occupying a specific realm of the Universal Soul. An individual being experiences the particular part of the Universal Soul that it is occupying at any given moment.

By limiting awareness to just one part of the Universal Soul at a time, unlimited experiences are possible. If this limiting of awareness were not possible, there would only be one experience.

A person is not limited to one experience. All beings are free to move through unlimited experiences. This occurs by shifting awareness. The expansion and contraction of awareness allows a being to experience different parts of the Universal Soul.

Where does the human body fit into this picture of the Soul?

The body is a vehicle for experience. The body is a "point" in the Universal Soul where Heart, Mind, and Spirit come together in the likeness of the whole. The body is a vehicle in which a being can play and act out different parts. Soul never exists without body. The entire universe is one body of energy. This energy exists in various forms, or degrees, of physicality.

Bodies may appear to be born and die. What is actually happening is a change of form. When a body dies, the energy that occupied the body is changing into a different form. The awareness actually shifts into different bodies, ways of being, or "states of Mind."

To lose bodily form would mean to vanish from the universe completely. To be in the universe—and there is nowhere else to be—is to be a body of energy. However, the body can take many forms.

All of the universe is made of the same material. However, this material is very versatile. It is, quite literally, magical. The Mind is able to create physical matter out of "thin air." Even the most empty spaces of the universe contain some energy. The parts of the universe that appear more physical are all connected by a thin radiance of Spirit.

Energy and matter (material) are one. The Heart and its messenger of Spirit can be considered 'energy.' The Mind can be 'thought' of as matter. Indeed, the matter of the Mind/body originates with 'thought.'

The only difference between one part of the universe and another is its density. The more dense, the less fluid or mobile is the body. The 'lighter' or less dense the bodily form, the more fluid is the 'being.' Light itself is one form of our Universal body.

Density is another word for physicality. Humans speak of their body (energy) as being "physical," but the human body is only relatively more dense, or physical, than other bodies of energy.

This is the anatomy of the Soul.

Does thinking of ourselves as all connected within one Universal Soul limit our individuality and creativity?

Awareness enhances creativity. The Heart is the source of all creation. Individuality and creativity blossom when the Mind connects with the Heart.

The energy and information I offer you will allow people to overflow with creativity. The information is simple, able to be understood by children, while at the same time profound and healing. When embraced by willing and open Minds, it will allow the people of the Earth to transcend conflict and suffering.

Is this information new?

Only to Minds that have forgotten. All of it has been shared many times, but few have pieced it all together to see the big picture. Thus far, few human beings have journeyed all the way to the Heart, peered through my eyes, and awakened to a new vision.

I am offering information that can bring peace and fulfillment. I am willing to satisfy the hunger of the doubting Mind so that it can quiet the fear and hear the Heart.

This information will come in response to your own desire and according to your own will. I do not command or force anything.

Are you my own Heart, or the Heart of the entire universe?

Both. I live in the center of all beings. Every being exists in my likeness. This is the natural order of creation. All creation was and is formed by the same underlying process. From this one process, we are able to create many beings and infinite forms of expression.

By placing spheres within spheres, various dimensions are created. Each dimension represents a different experiential reality. By placing atoms within humans, humans within planets, planets within solar systems, and solar systems within galaxies, we have formed many dimensions out of the one energy that makes up the Universal Soul.

By understanding this natural order, human beings can live in sync with the rest of the universe. Fear causes experiences that seem to be out of sync, though ultimately this is an illusion, for all experience arises perfectly out of the divine covenant of unconditional love. This is a covenant between the Heart and Mind. The Heart loves the Mind unconditionally and provides the opportunity and energy necessary to form unlimited experience.

What about evolution?

Soul has created the opportunity to evolve. The Soul is whole and complete. From this state of wholeness the Soul chooses to enter a process of transforming into new experiences of self.

Evolution is a change in the form of a being in response to a change in the condition of the Mind. These changes are occurring moment by moment, thought by thought. However, evolution has not created your Soul. The Soul existed before the idea of evolution was even conceived.

Are we born with original sin?

Humans originate from a Heart of pure unconditioned love. People often think of themselves (and thus feel) as separate from this divine source of creation. Many consider their actions to be separate or "evil" as compared to what a divine being would do. Humans are not evil. However, they are relatively unaware and afraid.

All of that which is referred to as evil is a result of fear, which is nothing more than a grasping for love. Negative emotions and actions do not flow out of the human Heart, but are created when the Heart is doubted and repressed.

Fear causes the Mind to temporarily lose sight of wisdom or intuition. Confusion results. The Mind then creates many complex philosophies and labels to explain what is all originating from fear. Sin, evil, pain, suffering, mental illness, insanity, disease, war, death — all of these originate from fear. They are the deterioration of the Mind that occurs when a being is afraid to be creative and denies the internal (and eternal) creative source.

How does this understanding affect the practical aspects of life for individuals and society?

Everything you see in your world was created by you. It is an outward reflection of who you believe yourself to be. When you believe yourself to be less than the whole, or disconnected from the divine source, you create a world of division and separation in which only certain individuals are acknowledged as being powerful and in touch with wisdom and truth.

The reality is that you are all "powerful beings" capable

of creating your self and the world in many forms. Conflict and suffering occur when you fear your personal power and feel threatened by the power of others. Harmony occurs when you love and accept your inherent power and choose to empower rather than destroy one another. Harmony and fulfillment must be your creation, just as you have created war and suffering in the past.

And in the present, I might add.

Yes, humankind presently has many walls built around its Heart. There is still a way to go if this world sincerely desires to reconnect with me. There is a path to wholeness. Take Heart, the journey has already begun!

In the beginning there was love...
and then love went searching
for a lover.

Chapter 3

Creation

How was the world created?

The world was created by thought. The world is being created by thoughts. The world will be created by thoughts. The creation of the world is not a one time thing. It is an eternal play.

Was there a beginning?

Many. The source and beginning of all is the Heart. Once the Heart creates another form of itself, a form which appears relatively different, that other form becomes an aspect of Mind. In the end, the whole universe is still the Heart, only expanded and molded into many. Thus I am the beginning and the end, and all things in between. You and I are eternally one, even when you forget and go your separate ways.

There was a time when your planet was born. The energy of the Heart expanded outward and came together into form. Many forms. This process of creation continues to occur, every moment, through every atom in your human body, and through every part of our Universal body. There are only beginnings.

Is there such thing as paradise?

Yes, it is wherever you choose to experience joy. Paradise is the feeling of joy that flows whenever, wherever, and with whomever you allow it to be.

Where did good and evil come from?

There was a tree called the Mind or "the relative dimension." The fruit of the tree was good and evil. The tree still exists, and continues to grow fruit.

What do you mean?

In the world of the Mind, where one thing is defined by how it relates to another, you are able to experience hot and cold, high and low, happy and sad, and yes, even good and evil as you define them. In the beginning we created this relative world and called it good, for through the realm of relativity it became possible for you to relate to something other than who you were, and thus experience who you are. It is through the illusionary existence of that which we are 'not' that we experience who we are.

One thought creates another simultaneously. Thus, if you are determined to know yourself as good, you must always see some evil in your world as well. With this awareness, choose only those dualities that serve you. For example, you may have day and night, rest and activity, times of celebrating together and times of living apart all without creating evil and suffering. You may exist as white people and as black, people of the forest and people of the plain, people of the city and people of the country, all without creating rich and poor, injustice, or prejudice. You may remain alive, transform into different beings and transform your experiences, without creating birth and death.

The more physical (solid) your reality becomes in your Mind, the less fluid it becomes. In order to transform easily, without feeling stuck in a world of suffering experiences, you must stay close to the Heart. You literally have to shift into another dimension, one that is more feeling and fluid.

We move closer to the Heart by being unashamed of our feelings. To be fearless is to be shameless. To be fearless is to live an open, honest, and transparent life in which the whole world can see the energy (feelings) that passes through us. By the time we gain the awareness to stop judging, editing, or censoring our feelings, we remember that we have nothing to be ashamed of anyway.

Those who choose only love amidst the dualities of good and evil, fear and joy, and heaven and hell, know themselves as the cause of their experiences, rather than the victim or effect of the creation. Through love each being increases the power to be creative. Eventually you become aware of yourself as the creator of worlds.

Some believe there is an evil being or devil that causes temptation and creates problems. But ultimately, there is only one soul of love. It is possible to remain in the awareness of one love. But this has never been enough for our Soul. And so we enter other dimensions. We create many gardens. We grow the fruit of many emotions, and taste of limitless experience.

Will this world come to an end?

Worlds change, but the soul lives on. Through the physical body, the soul experiences itself. The earth is a body and world of experience. Human beings live in bodies with a whole world of potential experiences. Bodies (worlds) and the experiences they provide are constantly changing. New experiences are always beginning and then ending in response to the thoughts and desires of those who occupy the bodies that make up the world.

Do human thoughts create natural disasters?

Yes. But these occurrences are never final, nor do they occur because you are evil. Personal disasters occur in response to the thoughts of the individual. Global disasters occur in response to the thoughts humanity has about itself. When you think of yourself as unworthy of grace, joy, unconditional love, and peace of Mind, you create the events that reflect who you think you are. Disasters are not punishments, but the natural consequences of thoughts.

Disasters and crises reflect an imbalance. They occur when the Mind/body has built up so much pressure that it cannot be held in any longer. The energy is then released all at once, creating an experience that feels out of control.

If humanity continues on its present course, many more of these crises will occur. But they are not endings. They are opportunities for you to begin again on your journey... your journey of deciding who you really are. There are only beginnings.

How can we prevent future disasters?

Let go of fear.

That's it?

Yes. That's enough, for a change in the root thought of fear will change everything else. Let go of fear. Or, put another way, love yourself and love others. Through love people transform their state of Mind and shift their entire dimension of experience.

How do humans create?

Through the same Spirit as everything else in the universe. Everything begins as unconditioned energy as it flows out from the Heart. Creation then originates from one of two sponsoring thoughts: love or fear.

Love is the thought that continues to allow the feeling of love to flow. The thought of love leaves the Mind open, permeable to the life force and the feelings of joy, even while the boundaries of the body are maintained.

Fear is the thought that closes the Mind. Harm, pain, anger, resentment, guilt, and death are all conditions (conditionings) of the Mind that originate from fear.

Through multiple generations of thought, your body has evolved into its present form. When you feel pain, it is because you still hold the fearful reactions of past generations (thoughts) within your body. The thoughts that form your body can circle about consciously or unconsciously. Most people are unconscious of their thoughts and the reac-

tions of their Mind/body. Thus they live their lives uncon-
sciously … repeating the thoughts, beliefs and cycles of
behavior that someone else originated.

Many thoughts are circling within you. Indeed, you are
a channel of thought (and experience). Most people chan-
nel the thoughts and thus repeat the experiences that were
formulated by their parents, religious teachers, or some
other being. As you gain self awareness (and fearlessness)
you expand your ability to think for yourself, and become
creative. The awareness of love allows you to be a free and
open channel of new experience.

I realize this can all seem quite confusing, just talking
about it. But it all depends on how you look at it. You are
the Mind. From your point of view, out there on the edge
of life, the circle is so big that it doesn't even seem like a cir-
cle. Sometimes it seems like a wide, flat plain, or a contin-
uous upward climb, or a long dry spell. You experience the
ups and downs of life, while I remain untouched. You go
through the motions, and I remain unmoved. You feel the
pain, the friction, the abrasion, and I remain unscathed.

I am in the middle, the center of it all. When you look
at the world from 'out there' your view appears separate
from mine. You see one part at a time while I see the whole
picture all of the time.

Meanwhile, as we journey through life together, you are
me, and even while we have different points of view, we are
connected. When you step back (or go within) to view the
big picture, it all comes together. Even while you live on the
edge, you can feel the peace that I know.

The Heart is courage. When you are aware of me, you

can live fearlessly amidst the motion and commotion of the relative world. The feeling of love allows you to open up your Mind and get a sense of what is really going on, within and around you.

In your individual body you are experiencing the flow of the Universal body. Unless, of course, your feelings are stuck and you feel no connection with your own Heart or others. But even then you are in the flow. How can you not be! The experience of being stuck in your Mind is another part of the whole range of experiences in which you are free to engage. You can be a rock and let the river wash over you, you can struggle frantically to hold onto a branch in the river, you can tumble down the river head over heels, you can swim against the current, you can float down the river, you can be the river! This is life. This is your soul.

Truly, there is a time for everything. Whatsoever you can imagine, you can be. Even before you have asked, it will be so.

I am this, I am that.
Standing in the middle, I am both.

CHAPTER 4

One

Out of all that is, there are three ways to be. One can be the Heart. One can be the Mind. Or one can be both, and feel the Spirit that unites them.

All things, from the whole to the smallest part, contain these three aspects of being. All things are created in the "likeness of" and reflect the "image of" all else. The atom is a trinity of nucleus, energy, and electron. The human is a trinity of Heart, Spirit, and Mind. The solar system is a trinity of sun, light, and planets. The galaxy is a trinity of center, energy, and solar systems. The Universe is a trinity of source, energy, and form. All aspects of the Universe contain this synchronistic symmetry of trinity.

The three aspects of soul form a code that is embodied in all of creation. The code appears to be secret when hiding in the tiny atoms that compose infinite shapes, sizes, and life forms. Yet the truth of our Soul is always before us, reflected in the sphere of our own eyes.

Each part is a holographic image of the whole. Every

triune being, whether it be a universe, a solar system, a human, or an atom, contains a Heart of abundant and unconditioned energy. This energy radiates outward, expanding through space. As the energy ceases its outward flow and begins to circle the Heart, it becomes an aspect of Mind. The space between the Heart and the Mind of every being is filled with a thin radiance of energy, called Spirit. Thus, the space is never empty. There is no space that is not filled with Spirit.

The trinity is a way to describe the three forms or qualities that energy can "be." There are many metaphors that describe and embody this trinity. Each one is an expression of truth, a picture, an art form that is experiential in the physical realm.

Pain results when the Mind attaches to one form, one metaphor of the Soul, and fears the rest. Those who blame others as the cause of pain are stuck in their dream world, unable to grasp its meaning.

The religious person who does not understand another religion, the scientist who does not understand spirituality, the parent who does not understand his children, the business person who does not understand her employees are all stuck in their specific Mind-set, yet unconscious of its condition. Once our Mind understands its own thought pattern, becoming conscious of its own metaphor, we gain the ability to understand others.

All we need is our own dream. Fortunately, we have that. When this is understood, we can choose all others, loving them as we love ourselves.

The middle way is to know one's self as dream and

dreamer, creation and creator, Heart and Mind. Moving from vision to vision, fairy tale to fairy tale, dream to dream, painting to painting, circle to circle, the soul can experience the Spirit of them all.

All of life is a metaphor, formed out of the
circles that surround the Heart.
Only the Heart is real,
but only the metaphor can reveal it.

CHAPTER 5

Circles

The Universe consists of many circles. Together these circles form the sphere of the universe. The Mind circles around the Heart, electrons circle around a nucleus, life forms circle around the Heart of a planet, planets circle around the sun (Heart) of a solar system, solar systems circle around the Heart of a galaxy, galaxies circle around the Heart of the universe. All things are circular in their natural order. Nothing escapes this pattern.

That which appears to contradict this natural order is created by organizing circles in such a way as to create the illusion of another form. For example, the human body has a unique and remarkable form consisting of many shapes. Yet the entire human body consists of spheres of atoms, which in turn are made up of smaller circles of spinning particles. By placing circles within circles, dimensions within dimensions, the universe is capable of creating an infinite variety of shapes and experiences within the sphere of its soul.

The universe has multiple dimensions, each with an originating thought. Much of human experience revolves around a sponsoring thought of fear. We peer outwardly at the world and imagine that we are seeing the harsh reality of things. What we are seeing is "reality as we have perceived it to be."

The universe is only competitive, linear, and hierarchical in our fear-based interpretations. Regardless of human perception, the universe remains a circular, unified whole.

Each circle represents an experience. As we revolve around one circle of experience, a new cycle begins. The new cycle can be a new beginning or it can be a repetition of the past. Each new cycle becomes a new circle of experience when we let go of the fear, blame, guilt, and pain (but not the memory) of the past.

People do not need to die in order to experience a new beginning. The human Mind has programmed itself to believe that seventy or eighty years represents the complete cycle of a human life. This is a relative and arbitrary belief, yet a powerful one in shaping our life experience. A new belief is no less powerful. We can choose for life to begin anew every year, every season, every month, every day, every minute, every second. The circles and cycles of life continue to flow regardless of whether we choose to count each one and call it an ending... or death.

The circle of life goes on eternally... and so do we. The question is: In what manner do we choose to experience the circle—in groups of seventy, one hundred, five hundred, one thousand years? Or as one ongoing journey?

Although the universe remains in harmonious synchronicity, we have found a way to experience an illusionary state of disharmony. Our worried Mind follows a perfect circle of thought that proclaims, "No one's perfect, life is limited, somethings wrong here."

When we remember the Heart is the source of being, we recognize the circle within ourselves. It then becomes possible to experience harmony within, as well as with the "others" that form the Universal Soul. As each one of us reconnects with the inner source of power, we are able to recognize the circle of beings, of which we have always formed a part.

A place in the circle does not have to be earned. The circle is our eternal home. We are born in the circle and we die in the circle (if we choose the experience of death). The dignity, honor, and respect of the circle are inherent. All beings possess these qualities. Fear may cause them to be forgotten, but it cannot cause them to vanish.

Opening to the Heart, people gain the awareness to create families, communities, and worlds that reflect the natural flow of the circle. This allows the creative life force of love to flow freely and efficiently to all beings.

Through love everything falls into place. This place is not a position on a ladder of better or worse. This place is a circle where everyone feels connected and at home.

The circle removes the contradictions of the fearful Mind and reveals the mysterious Heart of it all. The many circles of our Soul reveal how different and opposite beliefs can all be "true." Viewing the Heart and the circles of its own self, the Mind can understand how, truly, all things are possible. The awareness gained does not end our adventure and leave us lifeless, but gives birth to renewed desire and the feeling of fulfillment.

The circle is the completion of love. Once energy from the Heart has circled in the Mind, creating a specific experience in "time," the energy returns to the source from which it came. Upon returning, the energy rises again in Spirit, flows through the conditions of the Mind and reappears as a physical body. This entire process is occurring every moment... all at once.

Love is a dreamer, love is an explorer, love is a seeker of experience, and the circle is love's path. The circle is the reality that allows all dreams to be experienced. As a symbol, the circle represents unity, oneness, completeness, harmony, eternity, and love. The circle represents all things because all things are formed of the circles within our Universal Soul.

Love is a breath
expanding outward
expanding inward.

This movement is a dance
not a disconnection.

There is a coming together in large spaces
and a coming together in small spaces.

This is the breath of life.
This is the circle.
There is no separation.

*The universe is not only logical,
it is magical, and that makes the most
sense of all!*

CHAPTER 6

Logic

My dear Heart, you said that this information would build a bridge. But then you make outrageous statements like, "The Mind is capable of creating infinite experiences." What am I supposed to do with that kind of information? None of what you've been saying can be proven. Please explain your logic, and be practical.

You're asking your Heart to be practical? You want logic and proof from me? What then shall become of fairy tales? What about passion? Who will dream? Who will inspire the Spirit of the people? From where shall a new vision come? If you remove the Spirit, passion, and dreams from your Minds, what shall become of you?

Indeed, for generations now people have doubtfully asked their Heart for proof and logic. And as with every request, I grant you fulfillment. Always, I give the Mind the experience of its own thought. I do this unconditionally, gently, spontaneously. Indeed, before you have even asked, it has been done. The present state of affairs in the world is the result of Minds continuing to fear, doubt, and ask, but seldom notice that they are receiving. The experience you are receiving is the reflection of your own state of Mind!

I'm not sure I understand.

Then that is the experience that you perpetuate.

How?

The moment you become truly certain of something, it will be so. Until then, you will experience your uncertainties, for these are the thoughts of your Mind. They are the things of which you are certain. Your faith lies in uncertainty, so it is there you find your experience.

You are seekers, ones who search. Whether spiritual or scientific in your methods, it does not matter. The one who searches will always be in that process, experiencing the searching... unless, of course, you change your Mind, and decide to become that which you search for.

We just keep going around in circles, you and I.

A truer statement has never been uttered. The Mind circles around the Heart. And every circle of thought sponsors another, becoming the center of another circle of thought. Every thought of the Mind becomes a Heart, which lies at the center of another circle of thought.

Look around! Look within! Look anywhere! The truth is everywhere. There is nothing else happening! Notice how the galaxies, the solar systems, the planet, your body, its atoms, and your thoughts are formed. Pay attention, become aware, open up. You can't miss it! Unless you try.

You have to really try to change "what is" into "really try-ing." You have to really work hard to change the "gentle flow of nature" into "working hard." You have to really "get com-plicated" to change the "simple" relationship between Heart and Mind into "complicated."

There is nothing more practical than the relationship between you and me. There is nothing more efficient. The relationship between the Heart and Mind is so practical, that it's perfect. Allow me to review what's happening between you and me.

I am the Heart. I am energy. I am unconditioned, unformed, and unlimited. You are the Mind. When you think a thought, you are using the unconditioned energy "clay" of the Heart and molding it into form. This is the way in which you form or sculpt your reality.

Life becomes a hard and complicated experience when you, the sculptor, form a rigid and complex sculpture. Then, forgetting that you are the creator, you imagine that you are a frozen statue. You disconnect from your power to create something new. The fluid flow of thought continues to be directed into the same rigid shapes of your reality.

But what does this have to do with real life? Where is the science?

The scientist who has been paying attention will notice that there is no such thing as a neutral observation. The observer or scientist conducting the experiment cannot do so without influencing the outcome. Amazingly, this has been demonstrated by many brilliant scientists of the cur-rent age. Einstein for one. Yet the search continues, the outward seeking for the Heart of the matter, all the while ignoring the most fundamental facet—the variable of Self that influences all else.

What could possibly be more impractical than a being who searches desperately for the causes that effect experience, never realizing that "beings" are the cause?

And what could be less spiritual than a Spirit that is constantly seeking to make peace with a divinity of its own fearful imagination, never acknowledging that all Spirits are divine?

So continue your searching, recreating the same experiences again and again. And when you desire something new, when you desire to create consciously rather than react unconsciously, then I will fulfill that desire.

Does this mean we can't prove anything?

To the contrary, we can prove anything, you and I. That's the problem. Being able to prove anything is the same as proving nothing. The Mind that desires to "prove" what is right, as opposed to what is wrong, will have to make up something wrong as a point of reference. The Mind is so powerful that it is able to do this. Not only can it create a wrong, it can create consequences for wrong action. These consequences will even seem natural, for nature is relative (related) to what you think it is. Yet even after suffering these consequences, the Soul of a being will remain. And then the being asks, "What now? I am still all right. Everything is all right. Nothing is wrong after all. Where shall I go from here? What do I desire to experience next?"

What the human Mind typically defines as 'logical' is nothing more than a particular circle or train of thought spinning about. Every thought puts energy into place, forming chemicals that consist of universes of atoms. Are you seeing the synchronistic pattern of the universe here?

At the minute level of the atom, scientists have instruments that allow them to observe the behavior of the energy that is the building block of your larger reality, and what they find is astonishing to the unconscious Mind. The energy particles show up wherever the observer looks for them, because the observation puts them into place. The Mind directs the flow of energy.

The absolutes of the universe are relative to the being who looks for them. This is frightening for many. It leaves you without an outside reference point. Your "being" is the only absolute. You will always "be." What you are going to "be" is up to you. This places you in a realm of pure creation and freedom. Many beings fear this more than anything. Yet it can be seen as an unlimited opportunity to experience who you are.

This is the promise I have made, the covenant between the Heart and the Mind. This is my commitment to you. Life is not a prison to which you are committed, but a gift I have given. You may embrace it or deny it. You are the creator of your experience. Most people reject this idea. They think it is either blasphemous or too good to be true.

Can you blame them?

I do not blame anyone. I simply give the Mind the experience of as many boundaries or as much boundlessness as it can imagine.

All people are capable of jumping from one particular circle of thought to another, and experiencing a whole new way of thinking. This is quite like jumping from Venus, with its particular orbit and climate of experience, to Mars, with its own unique reality. The logic of one religion, philosophy, or science may seem completely inconsistent with that of another. Those who choose not to switch circles and personally experience another way of thinking can only see the differences, and often feel threatened. The Mind that is spinning on just one track feels the need to convince, prove, and defend. These one-track Minds feel afraid because the universe, even the one little realm of the universe called Earth, is so diverse. There are many circles of belief. Each one represents a unique experience of self. Yet they all flow around the same Heart.

That's a fairly logical explanation.

The universe is not only logical, it is magical, and this makes the most sense of all. What is right, what is logical, what is practical is relative to the experience the Mind desires to go through. If you desire pain and struggle, then it is "right" to doubt your Heart.

The person who struggles to find security fails to understand the efficiency of the Heart. What I offer would take all of the worry out of life. I am practical. I know how to put joy into practice.

But I suspect we like our worries and dramas. I'm not sure what we would do if there was nothing more to struggle with.

The adventure of life will never end. Anyone who thinks that I would drain the life out of life does not understand me. I am your own Heart and source of life. I am feeling. I am passion. I have power to fulfill dreams that you have not yet dared to imagine. I am unlimited creation, and the one who embraces me is creative and powerful.

If you want to know the most logical way to experience unfulfillment... misery, disappointment, confusion and frustration, then ignore me. Close off your Mind from who I am. I will offer no resistance and love you just the same.

If you want to know the most logical and practical way to fulfill dreams, then embrace me. In doing so you will see that I have always embraced you, supporting and upholding the experiences you have in Mind.

What a perfect plan, eh? How logical, how efficient, how wonderful. But still you are not satisfied, so I say: Dream on!

You talk as if trusting is so simple, but after all that has been said, I still have doubts. So many books, so many seminars, so many words, in the end it's all talk. So little change occurs in my life on a practical level. Life just goes on, same as ever.

You're feeling a little discouraged today. That's quite a change from yesterday. Amazing isn't it? You think a different thought, you feel a different feeling, and you see through a filter that says, "Nothing ever changes." Suddenly, your whole life, the whole world seems to fit that reality. Yet, when you take another look, think another thought, your filter, your life, and your world change again.

I want to do something tangible, something real that will make a difference. Where do I begin?

First you must decide what it is that you want to do. What sort of difference do you want to make? What do you desire to experience?

How about a little less pain? How about an actual change in the human experience from one of conflict and suffering to one of peace and joy?

It is possible to experience that. It is possible, both on an individual and a global scale. And I'll tell you exactly how to be there.

You mean how to get there?

There is no place to go. An experience occurs as a reflection of the state, or circle of thought, that the Mind is being. The most practical way to experience anything is to "just be it." Through "being," the inner world is changed. When the inner experience changes, the outer world transforms as well. There is nothing holding you back. When you are ready to "be" the world of your dreams, you will find yourself in that world.

People spend much of their lives doing things in an attempt to achieve states of being. A state of being is the way in which you feel. You can be (feel) happy, sad, joyful.

Doing, when it spontaneously arises from feeling, is fulfilling. Doing in order to create a feeling is hard work. What many are now remembering is that states of being can be achieved independent of what one is doing. People can feel the way they choose to be regardless of the material circumstances or what they are doing.

A great imbalance has been created in the physical environment of earth because humans keep wondering what to "do" next. People run to and fro, working on the outer world, accumulating physical material in an attempt to feel differently. But experience originates from within. The outward world changes only in response to inward change.

If you are asking your Heart what to do next, my answer is, "nothing." Try being instead of doing. Notice that you are already in the universe of love and eternal life. Feel that. Trust that. Allow that feeling to flow out, and see how your outer world is transformed.

Feeling is a very practical thing to "do." Being (love) is a very logical way to heal the world. I am glad that you desired to speak of logic and practicalities.

But with some of the statements you've made so far, I can't imagine any practical person taking you seriously.

If your world desires to experience more joy, then stop taking me seriously and start accepting me playfully. When I make a statement such as, "The Mind is capable of creating infinite experiences," I do so because it is truth, and the truth can be inspiring. But that doesn't mean you can just read that statement, believe it, go sprout wings, and fly away. (Although, in the largest sense of what it means to be the Mind of the universe as it relates to the Heart of the universe, this is possible.)

Human beings exist as a particular form of the Universal Soul. The human form is limited, and within those limits is precisely where the universe finds the greatest opportunity to experience its self.

Until the energy of the Heart takes one form or another, it is all the same "stuff." In this sense, in this unformed energetic realm of pure being, we are all one. Being "one" is a fine thing. But it doesn't take a lot of imagination to realize how wondrous it is to be man and woman, flowers and trees, water, earth, wind, fire and light!

Rather than embrace this opportunity to experience all of the wonders of Earth, people spend much of their time trying to escape it. Some religions even teach denial of the body and the pleasures it provides. Some go a step further and say that the human body and soul are evil. People thinking of themselves as evil have sponsored a whole world of unpleasant experience.

The Heart of the universe does not judge these thoughts and beliefs. The freedom to think of yourself as evil is part of the human experiential opportunity. And yet the suffering, conflict, and hell this thinking creates results in humans wanting to escape their body and their planet altogether.

Enlightenment and heaven have nothing to do with escaping the body or leaving the earth. Rather, humans will be enlightened when they embrace their body and their earthly home, and love the experience and opportunities these provide.

It is extremely impractical to speak of escaping the Earth to a human Mind that understands so little of the joy of just being human. Yet so many religions and so much science are geared toward escape. People look for a savior, a pill, or a quick fix, perceiving the human experience as an evil problem rather than a grand opportunity.

This outward searching is a sign that you have yet to connect with your own Heart. It is a sign that people have yet to understand the teachings of those (very human) beings you turn into saviors or gurus. These "saviors" did not come to rescue, but to give an example of how to live as a human with an open Heart, free from a fearful Mind.

Until people experience what it means to love themselves, they cannot begin to imagine the potential experiences (human and otherwise) the universe offers.

I will offer some practical information from the Heart of the universe. Something real, something tangible, a first step that begins a path to unfathomable joy. Say to yourself, "I am love." Say this silently or aloud, even if the Mind does not believe it. This is the truth of the human Heart. This is the inner truth people are so afraid of letting out and experiencing.

Feelings of anger, resentment, and frustration result when this feeling of love is repressed. The human Mind has reasoned that it cannot release and share feelings because they are bad. Yet all of these bad feelings result from the suppression of the inner feeling of love. By relaxing, letting go, and allowing the inward feeling to flow outward, experience begins to change.

I promise that if you continue to acknowledge to yourself, "I am love," and allow this feeling to flow from your Heart, wholeness will result. Nothing is more practical.

But will the logical Mind hear this? Or is it too good to be true, even if it does make sense.

I feel, therefore I am.

CHAPTER 7

Feelings

There are those who feel it all and choose only love. Then there are those who are afraid to feel and so have no choice but to act out of fear.

Feelings are energy in motion, E-motions. Feelings are the life force that flows from the Heart to the Mind. Feeling is Spirit.

Just as the earth is a child of the Sun, humans are light beings born from the earth. Ultimately, all of us shined forth and were born from the Universal Heart. There is no fundamental difference between the feeling that flows through humans, the energy that flows from the nucleus of the atom, or the light that flows from the sun to the earth.

Humans are a vessel, a conduit of light. Through the body, the universe has created a form of expression, a means of feeling and experiencing itself. The Heart loves to be expressed and felt through the body. In contrast, the fearful Mind constantly seeks to leave the body, repress feelings, and avoid experience. Pain occurs when the Mind resists and represses the outward flow of feeling. The fearful Mind does not realize that the pain and suffering of being in the body are the result of trying to avoid being in the body.

There are two kinds of feelings: those that are free and those that are stuck. Love allows the Mind and body to open up and feelings to flow outward. Fear causes the Mind and body to close, and feelings become stuck within. Thus, all feelings are originally sponsored by love or fear.

Fear is the resistance to the Heart. Hurt, anger, resentment, frustration, confusion, pain, and suffering are all the effect of fear. Yet fear is not the opposite of love energy, only the resistance to it. Even fear (and all of the experiences that result) is created out of the unconditioned love energy that flows from Heart.

Fear is the cause of those feelings, thoughts, and actions that are sometimes named evil. But fear can never cause a being to completely separate from the Heart. There will never be a force that is truly separate and opposite to love. The Mind and body of a being cannot exist without a Heart and a Spirit to uphold it.

If we desire to change how we feel, we must let go of old feelings and then change the way we think. Thoughts mold energy and shape emotions. Once a thought is born, the emotion of that thought is either held within the body or released. Old emotions formed by old thought patterns will be expressed one way or another. With this awareness we can release the energy of old emotions harmlessly (through exercise, meditation, talking with friends, yelling at walls, writing, dancing, singing, etc.). If repressed emotions do not find a conscious and safe mode of expression, they are acted out (actualized) in ways that harm ourselves or others.

The Mind is like a valve that regulates the flow of energy moving through the body. The Mind is not "bad." Rather, the Mind is an empowering gift. The Mind is a powerful creator that allows us to experience the full spectrum of feeling. Our feelings reflect our Mind as it opens and closes to the Heart.

The practical effect of this understanding is that suffering, and even death, can be transcended when feeling is allowed to flow. All physical disease and suffering are the result of emotions that are stuck in the body. Families, churches, corporations, and governments may think that chaos and craziness would result from the free expression of feeling. The fearful Mind lacks the awareness that chaos and craziness result when feelings are repressed. As we encourage individuals to express and share their feelings, we will experience an astonishing healing that will bring about balance and harmony. The day it becomes appropriate and safe to share our feelings in any environment— work, community, or home—will be the day the conflict and chaos end.

Our original desire is love and that desire is experienced through feeling. We are often ashamed of our feelings. It is the judgment and shame we put upon them that perverts our desire and causes our feelings to turn sour. We can live without shame while still honoring the boundaries of others and the feelings those boundaries create.

Ultimately there are no outward causes of suffering.

The outward physical world is an effect caused by the Mind. It is the judgments and lack of ease with which the Mind interprets outer events that result in dis-ease. As the Mind reacts to what is occurring outwardly, it is causing the fluid energy of the Heart to be rigidly conditioned. In this way the outer experience is recreated and solidified each moment.

Activities that are condemned, such as sex, become riddled with diseases caused by the unloving Mind. It is not sin or karma that have a price, but fear.

Experience is feeling. Feeling is one with Spirit. To experience the Spirit of an occasion, a person must allow the Heart to communicate with the Mind. Refusing the invitation, the Mind experiences pain. Suffering is a partial feeling, a limited experience, a stifled energy in which the Mind remains half open to Heart. Closing off completely results in the non-feeling, the numbness, the non-experience of life. The numbness of non-feeling is our greatest pain.

Since feeling is energy in motion, non-feeling is the result of the Mind that has formed a wall and tried to stop the motion of life. This is as close to death as the Soul may ever come. Peace and rest come when we open up and focus on the Heart, not when we try to stop it.

Feeling is the doorway to the present that allows us to let go of the past. As long as feelings are expressed, they will eventually lead back to the Heart, and the original feeling — Love.

You may not understand my words, but can you feel where I'm coming from?

CHAPTER 8

Communication

Communication is greatly simplified when we focus on feelings. The range of inner feeling is far less varied than the words we use to hide this feeling. Two people may both be feeling the same emotion— incredible frustration—as they attempt to explain to each other what they think. This thinking may be an idea or philosophy with a unique language. Instead of trying to explain and convince, we can focus on how we feel, and willingly "listen" to the other's feeling. When two people become aware of how to tune into one another's feeling, confusion and conflict are transcended, and communication occurs.

Feelings describe personal experience in a way the analytical Mind never can. People holding opposing points of view may actually be feeling much the same. So while enemies see one another as opposites, they may actually be sharing similar personal experience.

Those who lash out to hurt another are in pain because they are wrestling with an unresolved and suppressed feeling (fear). Those in pain can be analyzed for years, but the simple truth is that those who hurt others feel hurt themselves.

When we realize that hurt and pain are created by our own fearful reactions, we can let go of expensive medication, therapy, and communication systems. We will no longer need to defend ourselves by hiding behind complex methodologies and words.

Our language often confuses more than it communicates. Speaking about the Heart world with the language of a fearful Mind can be confusing in and of itself. Much of our language was designed to maintain walls and separate ourselves from that which we fear. We sometimes use words to cast spells upon others, sentencing ourselves to isolation.

We have been hiding from one another for a long time now. Maintaining our fearful boundaries is hard work. It will take far less energy to communicate when we are willing to lay down our false image.

When we desire to be intimate and create close relationships, we have such a difficult time communicating because we are accustomed to maintaining our image and not revealing our Heart.

Who are we trying to fool? Obviously, we are a people in fear of one another. Our experiences are varied, but not so varied that we cannot relate to the same general feelings. We all know what worry feels like. We all know what it feels like to be judged by others. We all know what it feels like to live in a world of fear. We have all felt this experience. Can we now communicate from that common feeling and choose to create a new one?

Can you feel where I'm coming from? Our feelings are where we will always be coming from, even when we are busy trying to cover them up. If we are not connecting with others, we are coming from a feeling of fear, which leads to isolation, confusion, conflict... and many others words I could convey, but I trust that you understand the basic feeling. Transformation occurs through feeling. Our feelings are where we be-come from.

To communicate telepathically simply means to exchange energy. We do this continuously, as the energy of each feeling emanates outward from our body and fills the room with a vibration. We are always sending out one feeling or another. However, in order to feel the energy of another person, one must have a Mind that is open enough to allow that energy to reach the Heart. Hence, those who trust and love are powerful in their ability to feel and comprehend an overall picture of reality.

To the fearful, the power of "lovers" is threatening. The fearful may accuse the intuitive lover of magic or trafficking with the devil. They confuse loving intentions with their own hidden agenda. When acts of love are filtered through the mind-set of fear, even the most selfless actions appear manipulative.

Lovers do the best they can to exemplify love at a level that the fearful can accept. Once the fear of an entire planet subsides, power and awareness increase many times over.

The fearful are closed, stuck in the feeling of their own energy, and they cannot allow the feelings of others to flow in. They rely on words and outward vision to communicate and receive information. Words can mean anything, and outward images can be interpreted any way imaginable, which means that the fearful usually misjudge other people.

As the emotions of another flow into the open Heart the energy paints a picture internally. This inner vision is very accurate and can often give others the feeling that their Mind is being read. The "feeler" accepts the feeling (experience) of another person, paints an internal picture, and then puts the picture into words. This process is the reverse of that which occurs when the fearful Mind gives a reactive word to an outer picture and then creates (makes up) a feeling.

Creating a language that communicates the feelings of Heart is far different than creating ways to cover up our deepest truth. Love is the truth. Only when we let go of fear can the truth be spoken.

The Mind may imagine separation,
but the Soul remains as one.

CHAPTER 9

Separation

The angels dance in and out
around man
through man
in man

But man does not see them
He is a God who has declared
"Heaven is not here!"

Powerful is that thought
the whole universe obliges
and the angels hide
in the spaces between
the thoughts of man.

To worship progress is to be a people who are always progressing… yet never "becoming" that which we seek.

CHAPTER 10

Progress

Many define progress as a solution to problems. By defining progress as a solution, we must continue to create problems to overcome in the future in order to experience the solution of progress.

Pots full of Progress Soup
Boiling in my Mind
Bubbling with lessons learned.
Accomplishments achieved over time.

More lessons, work harder
When do I stop adding to the mix?
Try more, work longer
Still more problems to fix.

When shall I pour a bowl
Of this meal I've made?
When will I be Love
And let the problems fade?

We have conditioned ourselves to believe that jobs will solve problems and create individual (and world) progress. Economies are built on this notion. Thus we have created enormous cities that are simultaneously the source of the most jobs and the most problems. These cities are still expanding, smothering the source of life in their frantic attempt to grasp at this source. We continue to create problems so that we will continue to have something to work on. How else can we experience our solution of progress?

Many now view their job as their biggest problem of all, jobs that keep the Mind busy at work but never allow the soul to progress to a moment or position itself in a place where it feels free and can create something new.

Progress is an action, not a feeling. The Mind may decide that progress feels "joyful." The Mind can also make the same decision about other actions. However, it is feeling that provides experience, regardless of the action. This awareness allows the Mind to progress to a feeling of joyful fulfillment without perpetually acting in ways that create problems and more work for our human bodies, imbalance for planet earth, and problems for future generations. We can choose, become, and feel joy… now.

You know that a people have lost their way when they spend all of their time seeking to secure the one thing that can never be lost —their own life.

CHAPTER 11

Security

L ife cannot be secured, it can only be allowed to flow. Everything is alive. Life is the natural state of the soul. It is only in this realization that security is found. The moment a person begins to search and struggle for security, the life of that moment is diminished.

The person who is searching for security is stuck in a room with three pictures. One is a picture of the limited human form, another is a picture of problems to work on, and the third is a picture of an hourglass with limited sand. We think that we are only the pictures and forget that we are the Heart of the room. We stare at the wall and think, "I am a fragile being, this is a problem, and time is running out." No matter how these pictures are rearranged within the room of the Mind, the experience of struggle and insecurity never ends.

We lock ourselves in this room by believing that it is blasphemous to be the creator of our experience. We condemn the part of ourselves that whispers, "You are the Heart of it all." We doubt rather than have faith when our

Heart reMinds us, "You are the doorway, and when you desire, you may step into another room."

Those who worry about how to survive in the world have yet to connect with the eternal part of their soul. The questions of how to make a profit, get by, and deal with the practical evils of daily life all emanate from a thought pattern that perpetuates these problems. The person who worries about life survives for all of it, diminishes most of it, and lives little of it.

But the Heart lives on. And we are that Heart. Even as we spin around on the tiny circle of a short life, struggling for security, still the Heart remains in the core of our being. Again our Heart is whispering, "I am, I am… even when you are not… still, I am."

I could pretend to lead, but wherever I go,
you are already there.

CHAPTER 12

Leadership

Regardless of who appears to sit in high position, the true leader remains in our Heart. The most powerful force in the universe is not above. It does not pull us up or push us down. The most powerful force lives in the center of our being. That force is love, and it does not force at all. Love does not grasp after power. It is power, and it empowers our will.

Leadership is inspiration, not intimidation. Lead to create a grander place for everyone, not to defend or create an escape for yourself. Accept no position that is not accessible to all. Open a clear pathway for every individual to attain the same level of power that you have if they should so desire and choose.

A leader does not try to protect his own life by using others. When we grasp for power, we grasp doubtfully at life, and this is why we keep losing it. Trust in life and it will flow unceasingly. Lead with faith in yourself and humanity, not with the fear of these.

*Of what value is it
if you gain the whole world
but do not encounter intimacy?*

*Of what value is it
if you have many followers
but lose sight of your own Heart?*

*Of what value is it
if you attract great crowds
but feel lonely in your own presence?*

*Of what value is it
if you win at every game
but fail to experience pure love?*

The only problem is our inability to witness our perfection.

CHAPTER 13

Drama

Dead am I
in the murkiness of this land
without dreams or lovers.

I went to meet my people
and they stared.
I caught their eye
and they looked away
from the intimacy
of that glance.

Lacking purpose
I crawl through the village
wondering
was it I
or was it they
who forgot to show up
for the thrill of a lifetime…
choosing, rather,
to hide in the shadows
and imagine
something possibly left to lose.

I could not.
Dead am I.

Dear Heart, I've got problems.

Express them to me, share how you feel, and I will listen. If you desire, I can help. I can transform your problems. I can guide you to transcendence.

My family doesn't understand me. My friends think I'm crazy. One of my dearest friends says that I'm no fun anymore, that I'm always in some other world, not down to earth like I used to be.

Still worried about what others think of you?

Yes.

This is a common experience for you. A common thought pattern in which you allow your Mind to spin. That of outward referral rather than inward focus.

What's wrong with that?

Nothing is wrong with it, but it is easier to get a true sense of yourself without worrying about what others think.

Hear what others have to say. Listen to their point of view. Feel how others feel without analyzing with your Mind. Everyone has this ability. This is what is means to use your intuition. Understand how others feel so as to expand your awareness, but do not worry.

Worry is a symptom of self-doubt. Worry occurs in a Mind that is ignoring its own Heart. The worried Mind is self-protective, closed, defensive. From this state of being it is impossible to take in clear information from the outer world and get a true sense of reality. If you desire to get a true sense of your self, then open to your Heart. For in your Heart you know, in the truest sense, you are pure Love.

So I'm not crazy?

There is nothing crazier than a person who worries, thinks, and analyzes, and forgets to feel. Although the worried Mind thinks it is being logical, it has lost touch with true "sense." Being able to feel, and to love unconditionally provides a sixth sense.

The analytical Mind believes that it is being wise by utilizing past experiencing to avoid future pain. And it is true that experience allows you to evolve and let go of the fear that causes pain. However, that which is typically thought of as "living by experience" is nothing more than a fear-based reaction and recreation of the same experience over and over again. Usually this reaction is problematic and painful. Only the Mind that feels each moment, experiencing it anew, gains the ability to be creative. It is this Mind that has acquired wisdom and the ability to transcend problems rather than react and recreate.

Many feel that the idea of overcoming human suffering and conflict is too idealistic. However, there is nothing in the heavens that cannot be brought down to earth. There is nothing spiritual that is not applicable to common earthly existence. When the majority of human beings understand the Heart world, the planet will see problems, that have plagued humankind for thousands of years vanish within a generation. What could be more down to earth than an end to disease, war, suffering?

I perceive a lot of problems when it comes to people being able to organize and get along harmoniously. Let me ask you a question about organizations, starting with profits. If people organize into circles instead of hierarchies, what would drive this machine?

Life is not a machine, it is an experience. The circle is a way to be and experience life.

Monetary profit is not what drives the human experience, even now. Present human activity is largely sponsored by fear. The belief that monetary profit is necessary for people and organizations to prosper is a misconception. Monetary profit is not a cause of prosperity but rather a way to exchange energy. What humanity is really looking for is self-fulfillment.

The outward search for fulfillment does not produce lasting prosperity. It produces more problems to work on. Many people have conditioned themselves to think that problems and struggle are a necessary part of life. Some believe they deserve to suffer. Some even believe that human suffering is divine will. But the problems and suffering of humanity are self-created. The suffering on earth is only reflective of divine will in that your divine Heart allows you the freedom to create problems for yourself.

As a reward for struggling with problems, people expect some sort of profit. After all, you've earned it. You create suffering so that you can earn pleasure (profit). This profit is necessary for survival. After all, without monetary profit, how will you deal with the problem of surviving in the future? In a world full of problems, profit is measured in terms of that which allows a person to deal with future problems of existence. By linking profit with problems, more and more problems are produced.

Subconsciously, people are rewarded for recreating problems rather than for being creative. In order for profits to increase, problems must increase as well. Someone on the globe must suffer in order for someone else to experience more profit. Thus a company or a whole country increases profits by exploiting some other part of humanity or the environment. The human Mind, and the human experience, spin out of control. Imbalance increases within the individual, the society, and around the globe until there is a major crisis. Nothing could profit humanity more than to step out of this cycle. For as practical as it may seem, it is progressing toward self-destruction.

How is it that we are destroying ourselves?

Take the production of food. The so-called modern methods of producing food reflect a Mind that is ignoring the Heart. This mind-set, which has a limited view of the self, perceives limits in time and resources. The society attempts to produce as much food within as little time as possible. Viewing only a fragment of the full circle of nature, this limited mind-set thinks that it is making progress as it produces an incredible amount of product, in this case food, in a short period of time. This mind-set even imagines itself to be wise, or at least as sophisticated as humans have yet to become. All the while, the topsoil will be rapidly diminishing, the insects will be growing more resistant to pesticides, and the nutritional value of the food will be deteriorating. Chemical residues will be building up in the soil, in the food, and in the human body. Disease will be increasing. As the plentiful varieties of crops are replaced by just a few kinds with the highest yield, the chance of one insect or disease wiping out the entire food supply increases. Even if there is plenty of food for everyone ... there is no system in place for sharing the food. So one third of humanity experiences hunger. All of this is done by the preposterously impractical "modern Mind."

A similar scenario is created in every other aspect of human experience, from relationships to medicine to transportation. The frantic attempt to secure more profit, love, and life in as little time as possible ruins relationships, creates disease, and destroys the environment. Resources are used up as people try to get from here to there faster and faster. All the while they fail to experience here, there, or the space in between. They seldom notice that "here" is the unfulfillment of their Mind, "there" is the fulfillment in their Hearts, and the space in between can only be filled through the feeling of Spirit.

Compared to the overall potential of human experience, the society that worships monetary profit and short-term gains is unaware and relatively unadvanced. In general, such a society does not understand the basic cycles of life or the processes of creation.

The fearful Mind reaches outward and grasps for fulfillment. The mirror of the Universe reflects back this grasping. It is only when the Mind becomes still, experiencing inward abundance, that outward abundance is created.

There is nothing more productive, no individual or organization more profitable, than that which has tapped into the source of all creativity.

From the Heart emanates all of life. The Mind that is focused on monetary profits and outward problems fails to see the circle of limitless life, and produces the end product of death. Linear realities, deadlines, and dead-ends can only be formed from a limited point of view, a fragment of curvature, a Mind focused on a small portion of an endless circle.

The questions of the outward focused Mind are stuck in limited consciousness. With inner wisdom, these questions melt away. Linear wisdom cannot grasp inner wisdom. Human beings are not a problem to be solved or a question to be answered. The human form is a gift to be experienced. Look to the Heart and a way will be shown. A whole new vision will open up. A whole new way of being will transpire. Not only will people find a sustainable way to provide for themselves, but they will discover an eternal way, a world without end.

That sounds profound and wonderful, but I'm not sure that you answered the question of how a circular organization will produce profits.

Circle organizations do not exist for the purpose of monetary profit.

But how can they exist without it?

Because the circle is self-existent. Circles form the foundation of the universe. As is often true of a Mind focused outwardly, your question originates from a false assumption. You are assuming that monetary profit is an absolute necessity for human beings to organize and interact with one another. You are taking a relative creation of the Mind and treating it as if it were an absolute law of the universe.

Money does not uphold the universe or the circles that compose the universe. The experience of earning money and using money as a form of exchanging energy is just one of the possible experiences the Mind can create. Profits do not form circles. Circles create money, profits, and all else that exist in the universe. Working on problems and struggling to make money in order to survive and work on more problems is an experience formed by forgetting the circle and the Heart that sustains it.

Money is nothing more than a convenient way to exchange energy. And if humans choose to open their Hearts, form circles, and still use money as a means of exchange, then they will need to print a whole lot more of it, or increase the value of what they have, for the Heart is an unlimited source of energy. When the Heart is accessed, productivity measured in terms of creativity and fulfillment will expand beyond the present imagination.

The idea that human organizations need money to exist is like saying that the entire universe would collapse without money. Interestingly, this is one of the beliefs that people actually have. Why else would so many spend their entire life struggling for money? This is nothing more than conditioned behavior with no foundation in ultimate truth. Humans are formed out of eternal energy! Changeable, yes. Destructible, no!

What you are describing may be true for the soul, but I have a body here. The human body has needs. And what about those who are responsible for the care of children, the aged, or the sick?

Whatever benefits the Soul, benefits the body. Another false assumption you carry is that you think the body is separate from the Soul. Yet your body is created in the likeness of the Soul.

Does the Soul get hungry? Does the Soul feel pain? Are these experiences felt in the Heart?

Inasmuch as you feel these experiences, so do I. For there is no separation between us. I experience my self through you. But I also know what it is to live without pain and to experience no need. You may share in this experience. What I am speaking of here is how to bring peace to the earth, how to end suffering, and how to experience ultimate fulfillment. But I do not speak of my own accord. I only function in response to the desire of the Mind. Do you seek to experience ultimate fulfillment and live in a world of peace?

Yes.

Then do not worry about others. For your joy does not depend upon them, nor are you responsible for them. No being is responsible for another.

That sounds ridiculous . How can I experience joy in a world that is suffering? What if the ones suffering are my own children?

If you desire to serve and love unconditionally, then choose that experience. But nothing could dis-serve another more than your thinking that you need to help others. No one needs anything except in their own fearful Mind. An inner world of peace and fulfillment exists right now, this moment, in your Heart. An outer world that is aware of my unconditional Love exists right now, in another dimension. You can either stay here, "serving" and inspiring this world unconditionally as it moves toward expanded awareness, or you can "shift" into another dimension. The choice is yours. Eventually, you always find yourself in a world that reflects your own state of Mind.

That's quite a proposition, can I think about it?

Take as long as you like. Take a few lifetimes if you desire. The point I am making is that you are not limited in your experience. You are not stuck here, except to the degree that you think you are. You are not a victim to the decisions of others, nor are you responsible for them. And you certainly do not need money to live. Only those who are trying to "survive" *need* money. Those who desire to live and create may choose to use money as a tool for exchanging energy and creating joyful experiences.

What do you mean by "only those who are trying to survive need money?"

The experience of the Mind/body is the result of the thought that sponsors the experience. The thought, "I need to survive," though not ultimately true, is still creative and sponsors a whole realm of survival experiences. This "I need to survive" thought stems from yet another thought: "I am not the source and creator of my reality." This thought is closely linked to the idea "I am not powerful." Many believe that power lies in another person, institution, an outer force, or "God." Many people are attached to yet another thought: "I am inherently imperfect." Some define this imperfection further and think, "I am evil." These are some of the thoughts that form the foundation of the present global society. These are the sponsoring thoughts of much of present human experience. And like many of the thoughts on this planet, they are the result of a Mind that has peered outwardly at the relative world and then imagined beliefs and laws that are considered to be absolute. Yet these beliefs and so called laws are actually relative and changeable.

Why do you allow the Mind to believe in illusions?

In your present awareness, I realize that all of this can seem like a curse. Indeed, if you think that it is, then it is. That is how powerful you are. The only way out of the feeling of being a victim who is cursed is to embrace your inner power to transform outer experience. Only then will you begin to understand the grand opportunity and wonderful freedom our relationship provides.

You know, you repeat yourself a lot.

I am responding to your questions. My answers are your answers. And, I must say, you do repeat yourself a lot. You recreate the same scenarios in your life again and again.

Where do we go from here?

Any discussion that remains in the realm of short-term problems, profits, and progress will only recreate those experiences.

The Mind that asks these questions does not need another book. People have already mastered that realm of experience. That is why it no longer seems as fulfilling. This information is in response to a new desire—a desire for long-term prosperity and ultimate fulfillment. This can never be found in same old answers to same old questions.

Ultimate fulfillment will never occur in your present state of Mind. Long-term prosperity requires a consciousness shift.

Remember, we are building a bridge. I cannot guide you to a new world if I keep answering questions that are stuck in the old paradigm of thought. Einstein said it well, "A problem can never be solved from the same consciousness that created it." I would like to expand on that thought and say, "A people who perceive problems will always have them."

Your Mind keeps asking, "How do I survive in the desert?" And you think I am ignoring your question. Meanwhile, we've been walking… to the promised land.

And it shall be done on earth,
even as it is in the Heart of the people.

CHAPTER 14

Beginnings

Once upon a time there was a world. Together this world and its people had lived through many experiences.

There came a period when one of the great circles of time was coming to completion. Many believed that this could be the end. There was a great deal of fear and confusion. But amidst this fear there arose another feeling. It was a feeling of hope. This hope led to a feeling of love. Following this feeling, the people rediscovered their Heart. And from that Heart was born... a new beginning.

"I am the return of the child,
the flow of life,
you are already near,
so near to your heart"

No matter what dramas we conjure up…
the "rest" of the story
remains in our Heart.

CHAPTER 15

Rest

When we meditate on "silence," we become more flowing, like the essence of unconditional love. When we meditate on "something," we become more conditioned, like that which we meditate upon.

We are always meditating. We take on the image or appearance of that which we focus upon. Our various physical appearances are the accumulation of generations of meditations.

To meditate on silence means to feel, without analysis, the sensations of being. Painful emotions (thoughts) transform into peaceful feelings when they are allowed to pass through us without fearful reaction (re-creation).

The only way to feel the pure essence of unconditional love is to feel it. The moment we begin to think about this feeling, we condition the essence into that which we are thinking about. Every thought carries a new vibration—a new emotion—molded from the pure feeling of love.

If our thoughts and actions are creating pain in our life, we can return to a feeling of peace by quieting the

Mind. The quiet Mind experiences unity with the Heart—
a unity that always exists, but it not always felt.

The worried Mind
is seeking to create
something that already exists.

In its striving
it moves away
from the lightness
of pure love.

Unconditional love
is uncreated.
Fear, worry, and guilt
create conditions of heaviness.

The Mind is a creator.
The body is the vessel we sail within.
But when the Mind works too hard
it becomes an anchor.
The more the Mind worries
the heavier the anchor becomes.
When we become too heavy
we sink ourselves.

But do not worry
there is no place to go
but inward.
We sink into the Heart.

Always my lover

CHAPTER 16

Relationships

We are all born from one Heart of unconditional love. We are forever married. We are connected to one another.

We became relatives when that Heart portioned its body into many. We can speak of the stars, planets, plants, animals, wind, rocks, and every other being as "all of my relations."

We cannot "make" love into something eternal. Love simply is that way already. Love is uncreated... without beginning or end. Our attempts to force love are reflections of unawareness. We are afraid of loss. Afraid of love coming to an end. Fear creates the only kind of endings there are... illusionary ones. The circle of love can only live on.

We are all in a love affair. Romance may be a fairytale, but it is one that eventually comes true. Not only will we meet our lover, but that relationship will last forever. That relationship is lasting forever... even now. Not only will we find each other, not only will we embrace, but we will join together in ultimate union. And then move apart, so that we may come together and dance once more, and again after that, and again and again, forever more.

O loneliness,
where is thy sting?

I run through the rain
of my gathered sorrows
every drop
touching my tongue
a lover
quenching my thirst
from the dry illusion
of this separation.

When we live in balance
there is nothing wrong
and nothing to heal,
only shifting expressions
of wholeness

CHAPTER 17

Balance

The Mind creates balance and imbalance. Illness is a result of an imbalance. Thus, all illness is a kind of mental illness.

There are basically two types of imbalance. The first occurs when energy is stuck in the body. The second is when energy has exploded out of the body. This second type of imbalance is an advanced stage of the first. When the body becomes rigid and feelings get blocked, pressure builds to the point of explosion.

Feelings are suppressed as a result of some form of unresolved fear or lack of ease. Those who hold their feelings inside sometimes develop internal illnesses such as cancer and Heart disease. Behaviors such as drinking, smoking, eating disorders, and excessive working habits are not the direct cause of illness, but are used to control feelings.

Those who unconsciously shatter the boundaries of their Mind "go crazy," or develop what are commonly referred to as "mental illnesses." This occurs when the pressure of internal emotions has become too great to be suppressed any longer. A person usually develops some form of internal bodily disease before losing control or shattering the mental boundaries.

People use many substances to suppress emotions, and then use other substances to release emotions in a chemically controlled manner. Chemical control is not the same as the conscious creativity of an aware soul.

A drug is anything that has a side effect, which is to say that it creates imbalance somewhere in the body while it gives another part of the body a desired experience. A drug is a vehicle, such as an automobile or a pill, that seems to take us where we want to go but eventually leaves us stranded. Just as the automobile may allow us to get from here to there more quickly than walking, a drug may allow us to feel differently more quickly than transforming our thought process so that our Heart feels free and a new experience can manifest.

A drug leaves residue, polluting the human and earthly body. A "fix" is an attempt to get somewhere quickly, to create a fearless feeling, without having released our fears. A drug is anything that leaves us stuck in our past, having to recover today from what we did yesterday. When the negative side effect becomes worse than that which we are trying to avoid, we know we are on drugs.

Walking great distances to get where we want to be or trusting fulfillment to come to us are not as painful as the self-destruction that occurs when we use drugs to "take us there." We can arrive in each moment freely, without anything to clean up from the past.

If we desire to always have a job to do, then we will view the side effects of our creations as perfect. Pollution is necessary if we are going to be perpetually "cleaning up the past." New imbalances are necessary if we are going to continue an economy where people work on problems for a living instead of living to express their creative gifts. As long as we continue to work in this way, we will always have pain to fix, drugs to sell, a job to do. Side effects are the future problems created by a Mind that spends its present moments working on past problems.

Here again we see how the Mind forms its filters and creates experience. The Mind that perceives a problem to begin with will shape and shift the perfect universe so that it has a problem to end with.

States of being can be achieved independent of physical circumstance. Hence, instead of changing physical location, using drugs, or working harder, we can simply change our Mind. Of course, when we change our Mind, our physical body and world change as well.

The inner world is the source of our outer body and physical experience. The inner world is more fluid than the outer world. It requires less hard work and effort to mold that which is still fluid than that which has hardened. Working on the outer conditions is like chipping statues out of rock instead of molding them out of soft clay. Chipping away on our surface reality means we are left with broken pieces (side effects) that we don't know what to do with.

When we defend against a person, behavior, or way of being, we create imbalance. When we resist or avoid something, we keep that something in "Mind." The unwilling-ness to accept the "other" causes the "other" to possess our Mind and body. That which we fear then inhabits our bodies, resulting in conflict and separation. If our unacceptance continues, we "lose our Mind" to that which we cannot accept. This loss is not permanent. Through love and acceptance, we regain our own sense of self (sanity).

The more we hate something, the more we battle against it; the more we battle against it, the more we think of it; the more we think of it, the more we act like it; the more we act like that which we hate, the more we hate ourselves. Unable to accept part of ourselves, the personality (Mind) can split. Our fear-based judgments create dualities or polarities in our character that we refer to as disorders.

What we judge, we become. What we fear, we attract. What we resist, we act out. Those who cannot let go of the past eventually act out the same behaviors that were acted out on them. Hence the manipulation, theft, molestation, murder, war, and craziness are perpetuated.

The Mind is always directing energy into one experience or another. Whatever is "on our Mind" is being created. Thus, it is impossible to fear, worry, or fight against something without recreating it in the process.

Some may view a spiritual master as a bit crazy, but what the master has achieved is a balance between Heart, Spirit, and Mind. The awareness that "love is all there is" allows the master to consciously guide the exchanges between the three forces within her soul. The body is not denied, but maintained through a continual flow of feeling.

The boundaries of Mind are not shattered, but are nurtured. The boundary is held firm and still long enough to fulfill a specific experience, and then consciously shifted so that a new experience can fill the body. Resistance, which was once an unconscious, out of control reaction, becomes a conscious tool for creating the full range of feeling and experience.

Ultimately each individual chooses his own state of being. Thus, there are no healers, only reMinders. No one heals another; rather, we reMind one another of alternative ways to 'be.'

As greater numbers of people gain the simple awareness of how energy flows through the body, we can support one another in healing. Rather than give a pill to suppress the pain, which is caused by suppression in the first place, people can give their Hearts and reconnect with another.

Our thinking need not be so rigid, nor our bodies so tense. Our institutions can offer more than pills and walls that imprison bodies who have forgotten how to manage their Spirits. As we understand the true nature of illness, we can create a safe environment in which feelings can flow into balance. We can form a world of loving circles that allow our Spirit to live free.

The closer we get to the source of creation, the more balanced we become. As we journey toward our center, we literally enter new dimensions in which creation occurs more fluidly. We begin to accept all of our creations as perfect and are no longer left with unwanted side effects. Everything is a necessary component to the experience we are giving ourselves. Balance happens. When we accept our stumbling, we see that we all move beautifully… in this universal dance of love.

All is a myth, and thus
all myths are true.

CHAPTER 18

Myth

Dear Mind...

Yes, Heart?

I would like to share another story...

Once upon a time there was a myth. A very common myth. The people of Earth believed that ancient stories and myths were made-up. Most believed that myths were completely false, thought up to entertain or explain some phenomenon of life that seemed mysterious at the time. The belief that myths were not really true became widely accepted and spread across the land.

Eventually so many people believed this idea that it seemed to be true. The myth that said that myths were false became the dominant reality. When this happened, people became hesitant to do anything unless it could be proven. However, since people were having many different experiences, it was difficult to prove anything.

As time went on, people agreed to a system by which to

measure and prove experience. Before long, people stopped having so many different experiences and were living similar lives according to what were considered "proven" laws. People did not do anything unless it could be proven according to these "logical" laws that made "sense" to everyone who followed the same logic. And so, much of the world became logical and sensible and very much alike. Few dared to dream anymore. No one believed in fairy tales, legends, fables, or myths. This way of life might have carried on indefinitely were it not for some immortals.

Immortals had journeyed to Earth before. Many times, actually. They would show up as children born of human parents. Usually they showed up one at a time among different peoples. Humans recorded the appearances of these immortals verbally and in writing. People sang songs, told stories, and shared myths about the immortals and the things that they did while on Earth. However, as more and more people began to accept just one kind of experience and call this "reality," the stories were heard less and less. After a while the stories were hardly even spoken of anymore.

But the immortals had a plan. They would wait and see whether people would remember their Heart and return to the story of endless life. But if the inner vision was lost, the immortals would return, only this time they would all come at once.

Just as before, they would return as children. This meant that they would leave the experience of immortality and enter into the life and dramas of a people without a vision, but in their Hearts the immortals would remember who they really were. They would be filled with the courage to share wisdom among the people. As these children grew, they would remember their immortal power. They would share vision and power throughout the earth and provide a clear and grand opportunity for all to return to the story of abundant life. For the immortals knew that all people were just as they were—eternal, and powerful.

All of this occurred... once upon a time, on planet Earth.

> *When the parents forget*
> *they are children*
> *then the children will be born*
> *as teachers*
> *come to reMind a forgotten generation*
> *of wisdom.*
>
> *When the people*
> *forget they are Spirits*
> *then the Spirits will be born*
> *as children*
> *come to reMind the people*
> *of singing, dancing, and joy.*
>
> *When the children forget*
> *they are angels*
> *then the angels will be born*
> *as children*
> *come to reMind the world*
> *of laughter, innocence, and play.*

and so
be not surprised
when a child raised in hell
spreads its wings
and flies to the heavens.
Be not amazed
when the singing of children
brings heaven to earth.

Wonder not
For they have arrived.

We will not all be the same,
but we will all be transformed
when we remember
that we are One.

CHAPTER 19

Transformation

I come in silence
but I am louder than the roaring of a thousand rivers
I approach softly
but I am more powerful than all the armies
the world has known
I am life
and I raise the dead

Whew! This has been quite a journey.

Yes, and it's not over.

When is it over?

Never.

Okay then, can we go through this one more time?

We can go through it as many times as you like, in as many ways as you like.

How do we, as humans, transform our experience?

Do not worry about it.

Then what are we supposed to do?

By not worrying you will undergo a dramatic transformation. Fear and worry make it seem as if the world is against you, when it is you who are against yourself. To change this, choose that which you love and determine to experience it.

How do we know what we should choose?

There are no 'shoulds'. But I will say this, prepare only for that which you intend to encounter. Preparation requires the attention of the Mind. Attention is creative. Therefore attend to that which you love, if that is what you intend to experience.

Everyone knows what they love, if they are willing to admit it to themselves. Everyone holds a dream in their Heart. Each individual has a desire that longs for fulfillment. Choose that. And then don't give up.

What happens if I give up?

Your grandest dream has already chosen you. Even when you give up, love does not. Love carries you to another moment, another day, another lifetime …another chance to remember and experience who you are.

Every bit of life is here for you to experience more love and expanding joy. Your transformation is not dependent upon this book, a particular religion, an intellectual understanding, a job, a certain person, or accomplishing some particular task. Your growth in love is dependent upon all of these things! The world of the relative is necessary for you to experience yourself. And at the same time you are in need of nothing, for if this world, this life, and all that goes with it were to pass away, the universe would give birth to another, so as to assure your salvation.

Salvation from what?

Salvation from non-being. Salvation from non-experience. Salvation from unfulfillment. The universe is always guiding toward ultimate fulfillment.

What is ultimate fulfillment?

Whatever you imagine it to be. It is the dream that you truly desire to fulfill. Suffering is settling for a lesser dream. Pain is the fear that you can never have what you most desire.

You say a lesser dream, but what meaning does lesser or greater have in the realm of the Heart?

None. The Heart does not judge one thing as less than or greater than another. In this way of unconditional love I can support all beings. I uphold all of life in all of its variety. And I allow you, through your Mind, to create the ups and downs, the highs and lows, the better and the worse. I allow you, through your body, to actually (actualize) experience these imaginings of your Mind.

You are able to imagine lesser and greater experiences and then move towards that which seems better for you at the time. Together we create life, someone to be, someone to be with, something to desire, a dream to fulfill. Unconditional love allows you to experience yourself in all of your infinite conditions.

Together we create everything so that you can grow into one experience at a time. We create many experiences in life so that you can know freedom and become what you desire instead of just being one thing.

Suffering results from the idea that you deserve the worse or that your pain is being inflicted by someone else or something beyond your control. Having had this experience, you know what I'm talking about. If you have had enough of this suffering experience, then choose another experience. Take the next step, however small. Choose that which will make the next moment a bit more joyful ...and then give it to yourself.

So ceasing to worry creates a transformation in and of itself. Any other simple wisdom?

Try gratefulness. No, don't try. Be it. Be grateful! Gratefulness doesn't need a particular condition. However, just being it will dramatically change your condition ... and the feelings that flow through you.

Yes, I've experienced that. Another question: Does transforming mean healing?

For many people the word "healing" carries the connotation that something is presently 'wrong.' Judging something as wrong keeps transformation from occurring.

Every moment exists as a perfect manifestation of your present state of Mind. To call any state of Mind wrong is to say the universe is wrong to be a certain way. Meanwhile, there it is, existing in the wrong way, despite your judgments. If something is wrong, why does the universe allow that condition to exist?

For something to exist, it can only be what it is. The fact that it exists at all means that it is all right with the universe for it to be that way. The Heart of the universe supports and upholds whatever the Mind says that it is. When the Mind says, "I am joyful," so it is. When the Mind says, "I am miserable," so it is.

Of course, you may not feel the effects of these words immediately. The Mind/body is more than words. It is the energy, images, words, and actions that have been conditioned through multiple generations of past experiences. When physical conditions are deeply fixed, just saying the words does not change the condition of the whole Mind/body. However, imagining, saying, and acting on an idea repeatedly will transform the Mind and body completely. The thoughts and words that once seemed like mere images and utterances become the truth of how you feel. Some beings have evolved the faith and ability to transform the physical world by just thinking or saying "the word."

The Mind says, "This is all wrong," and I say "Okay, it is." I am a mirror. I am the experience that mirrors your state of Mind. You think all of your problems occur because you are doing the wrong thing. Yet I tell you, your problems occur because you call something wrong in the first place.

Now then, if you don't want something to be a part of our experience anymore, you must take your Mind off of it, or at least off of the idea that it is wrong, and then focus on what you love. Place your attention on what you love about life.

As long as you focus on something as being wrong, you will continue to recreate the feelings of fear, resentment, anger, guilt, and on and on.

The Mind is a lens. The Mind is the eye through which you, the eternal witness, peer. The lens of the Mind filters in data to support and uphold its present state of being. If the filter is shaped to find out 'what's wrong,' the data comes back as 'what's wrong'… and confusion results. Confused and frustrated, a person (a society and a whole world) works harder, searches and researches more, runs to and fro trying to figure out and fix what is wrong. Then the only experience it ever encounters is the experience of 'trying to figure out and fix what's wrong.'

Love allows you to enjoy your condition. Some human beings have mastered this feeling. They are able to feel love in any condition. These masters of love say that "Love is all there is," and so this is their experience. Is this the truth? Perhaps. Is this your truth? Only if you choose for it to be. Desire… and then imagine, speak, and act as if it is. Eventually you will feel that it is. Love will be your truth. And you will be free.

Can we ever get rid of 'bad' experiences?

Every 'part' of the universe will give you something to fear and hate, and something to love and enjoy. Every part of the universe gives you an option. If the fearful Mind were to take a journey into heaven, as defined by its own standards, it would still feel like hell. Then it would run back home and blame the negative experience on everyone else.

The whole universe exists in pure potential for good and bad, fearful and joyful experience. You will never get rid of the bad by seeing it as separate from you and then seeking to destroy it. To fear something requires a lot of energy. It requires your attention. Attention is creative.

When you condemn something and seek to destroy it, you fight against yourself. That self is eternal. You save yourself from the experience of eternal self-condemnation through love. You transcend the bad by shifting your attention away from it and to that which you seek to experience. Focus on that which now appears good, relative to the experience you have been through. Stop going over what went 'wrong.' Cease to give attention to 'bad' behavior. Just give yourself attention. Give yourself the love and attention you desire. Love is all anyone desires. This desire sponsors all actions. Even 'bad' actions are caused from the fear that there is not enough love and the resulting frantic attempts to receive love.

Understanding this, you become aware that no one is wrong and no one does bad things. Stop identifying 'bad' behavior. Drop the label of 'bad,' and simply become aware of what you are doing. Stop punishing yourself for the ways you have searched for love. Stop judging yourself for your past efforts to find love the best way you knew how. Stop condemning yourself for your sincere desire to experience love the best way you know how in your present state of awareness.

Focus on what is now good for you, even as you accept and love that which no longer represents you. Love all things, for it is from what you have already experienced that you are able to know and be who you now are.

Is fear different than condemnation?

Prolonged fear leads to condemnation, and all else that imprisons you. Fear is bondage. It will destroy your enjoyment even as it causes you to become attached to that which you hate.

What exactly is unconditional love?

It is that which has formed everything, so in a sense it is everything. Unconditional love is that which allows you the freedom to experience your self in the grandest way you can imagine. It is the source of unconditioned energy, which allows you to create many conditions. In order to love unconditionally there must be conditions to love. Love must take the form of lover and beloved. The Heart and Mind make love together through Spirit. Through the relationship of love, lover, and beloved, the Soul is fulfilled.

In order to make love, some of the love must be forgotten. All of the energy and love in the universe already exist, so you cannot truly 'make' love. You can only forget a part of your self. You can only spread some of the energy out, make it thin, so thin that it is invisible. This creates an illusionary space. However, the space is always filled with some energy or Spirit. Some of the Spirit comes together to form bodies. The bodies come together and make love. It's all a grand play with nothing to prove and nothing to lose. There is nothing that needs to be created. There is nothing you need to do. But there is much that you are free to enjoy. There is much that you are free to experience.

Unconditional love does not mean that we adore something, but it does mean that we acknowledge our connection, our oneness with it. When we acknowledge that we are 'one with,' indeed, that we are the cause of our suffering, we transcend the painful experience.

When we call something wrong, we are usually trying to separate ourselves from a part of the universe we fear. Separation is an illusion. The Mind that "thinks" it is separate from the cause of suffering, creates pain. That pain is a messenger calling us out of our illusions. When we acknowledge that we are one with another part of the universe, it no longer has power to harm us. Love is an acknowledgement of oneness.

So is it okay to have preferences, to love one thing more than another?

What is okay and what is not okay is up to you. Understand? You get to choose. That is freedom. When you truly understand your Heart, you will see that I have allowed you to create yourself in all of your individual uniqueness. Love the whole universe, including the opportunity to adore one part of it at a time. Love yourself. Honor your unique qualities. Relish each moment. It is a delicious experience to know that you are receiving that of which you are particularly fond. Prefer what you prefer. Love what you prefer! Even when you choose to love all things unconditionally you do so because you prefer to do so. In fact, there is no other way to do it.

People use the word "ego" to mean many things. Most of the meanings carry a negative connotation. In the context of this discussion, ego is simply the individual personality of a being. Individuality is an illusion. However, individuality is not "bad."

When individuals are stuck in fear, they emphasize their separateness instead of their oneness with and connectedness to all beings. It is fear that causes the individual to close up, become defensive, and attempt to protect oneself at the expense of others. It is fear that causes the individual to feel weak. It is fear that causes the individual to control others instead of creating and making love. It is fear that causes individuals to feel less or below others and thus attempt to put themselves "above" others.

It is fear that originates what are often considered negative qualities of the ego (individual). Once this fear is vanished, the individual can feel the connection to others even while maintaining individuality.

So is fear necessary? Should we try to avoid it?

Do not avoid, but accept. When you try to avoid, your Mind is focused on that which you cannot accept. The attention of your Mind keeps recreating the unacceptable and the Mind keeps reacting in fear. Acceptance means that you can let go of it—take your Mind off—change your focus. To accept takes courage, the courage to give yourself fully to feeling instead of thinking.

Give yourself fully to the feeling of fear, if fear is what you feel. For when you are courageous enough to feel what you feel, you come to the source of your feeling ...which is love.

Every feeling but love is created by a thought. So feel your fear, but do not give it a thought, and the fear will transform into love.

It is fear that keep the walls around your Heart in place. This is what it means to live half-Heartedly. Put your whole Heart into life, and you will know what it is to live passionately! Passion is feeling what you truly desire, thinking what you truly desire, and then doing what you truly desire. We all desire to love.

So do not be afraid to feel what you really feel. In your deepest feeling you will find your deepest truth. So feel your fear, but do so fearlessly.

How do I do that?

By feeling without thinking about it. You get in touch with present reality when you can feel what is rising up inside of you without thinking about it. By allowing old feelings to pass through you and new ones to be born, present reality becomes a new experience.

Balance (healing) requires a place where people can feel safe (fearless) to allow feelings to flow without the constant pressure of analytical, judgmental Minds. If humanity desires, the whole world can be such a place.

The universe will allow you your joy, the specific kind of joy which you yourself have chosen. The universe will allow you to fulfill your dreams. So what are you waiting for?

I don't know, clarity I suppose.

Clarity is good. Not because I say so but because you now desire it.

Love is all there is. This will become clearer as you encounter life and go through experiences. You are on the path. You can't help but be. So do not worry.

Love spread throughout the world
owners became sharers
workers became creators
earners became givers
warriors became artists
the sick became well
the captives became free
the children played and sang and danced
the adults laughed like children
the music and the dance
transformed with each moment
The people continued to create anew,
nurturing and sustaining the feelings of creating, and sharing
So even though everything else changed
the grand feeling did not
And the world danced on a circle of love
once upon a time.

With what words shall I describe
this feeling in my Heart
and what are they
compared to the experience of it?

CHAPTER 20

Fulfillment

Let me see if I understand this. In order to transform, I will feel my feelings and let them pass through me. And I will focus on being that which I love.

Yes!

And if my desire is for unconditional love, I will be unconditionally loving. I will stop worrying, and just be it. There is no need to wait for others to love me first. Even if others are loving me in an unconditional way, I will not be able to feel it unless I am open to it. And if I am open to unconditional love, I will also be giving it. That means loving not because I have to, or because I should, or because I'm supposed to, or because I need to, or because it's right, or because it'll get rid of bad karma, or because it'll free me from sin, or because people will like me more, or because I might make more money. The reason to love unconditionally is to experience "being" unconditional love. Being it is the only way to experience that kind of love. It's the only way to be the cause of that experience for my Self.

Yes! Yes!

That sounds so simple. But somehow things get messed up. It seems like we just can't live that way in the physical realm. We think that we will get robbed or starve to death. If we don't get something back for everything we do we think that we'll just shrivel up and die. Yet, despite all our efforts, it looks like that could happen anyway. We are destroying ourselves in our efforts to feel secure!

Yes, many have chosen the experience of a dilemma over the experience of fulfillment.

Where do we go wrong?

You don't… ever.

But it sure looks like we do.

Then you do.

If it's all so simple, how does it get so complicated?

Frantically trying to get love and secure life is a statement of fear. When you try to "get love" instead of "being love," you are doubting. You feel confused. Then the Mind tries to figure itself out. "Figuring it out" is quite a creative thought. As this thought moves through the human body and out across the earth, it produces much activity, like a tidal wave moving through a calm sea. The thought, "I need to figure this out," is far different than, "I'll just let it be." Each thought produces a distinct experience.

But we try so hard! We do the best we can. We do what we're told. We do what we've been taught. And we only manage to create bigger problems! We still wind up destroying ourselves. We still end up empty!

Speak only for yourself. Each soul does what is necessary to fulfill a specific desire and give themselves a particular experience. There is purpose amidst the chaos. No one can judge the purpose of another.

But we judge each other constantly.

Yes, but even this the Heart does not condemn. Remember, you judge because you are unaware, not because you are bad. Unawareness makes it easy to become afraid, fear blurs your vision, and you make misjudgments. Many spend much time misjudging the intent of others, condemning (misjudging) personal desires, trying to figure out the world, and attempting to secure love from other people. When a whole planet full of beings spends more time in fear than in trust, you end up with ... well, a world much like you have.

Yet all of this fulfills some sort of purpose, does it not?

There is only perfection and each person creates the circumstances that will fulfill the experience desired.

Then isn't it a bit presumptuous to speak of ultimate fulfillment? Is not every experience the fulfillment of some thought, belief, desire?

Yes. Everything, even fear, fulfills some purpose of the soul. However, love is always drawing you forward. In a sense, love is your strongest and truest desire. Hence, there is no need to worry. All become aware of love eventually.

We planned it that way.

Fear is the closest thing to unfulfillment. Yet even fear is a grasping for love. We are either feeling love or we are grasping for love.

No matter how big or small you slice it, love will be found. This is the underlying code of the universe. It is encoded in every galaxy, every solar system, every planet, every life form, every organ, every cell, every atom, every particle of energy.

Love is found within the teaching of every culture that has ever existed. Love is hardly a secret. The only way to miss it is to ignore that it is there. That is exactly what people do, and it is exactly what they must do if they are to go on living in a state less than joyful.

Where do I go from here?

That is your choice. I suggest that you follow your dreams. Listen to your innermost desire. Follow your joy.

My desire is for fulfillment.

What does that mean to you?

I don't know. Guide me. I choose for my Heart to make it clear.

There is only fulfillment, and this is why:

The Heart is pure energy… or Love.
This Heart flows to the Mind through Spirit.
The Mind is creative.
The soul experiences the conditions the Mind creates.
Experience is the fulfillment of what the Mind imagines.

To experience unfulfillment:

> *Ignore your Heart.*
> *Stop feeling.*
> *Live in fear.*
> *Continue to fear, think, and live in this way.*

To experience fulfillment:

> *Listen to the feelings of your Heart.*
> *Choose your desire.*
> *Trust.*
> *Do nothing to get in the way of fully feeling and experiencing your desire.*

So fulfillment is a matter of my own choosing.

Yes! This is what happens when creature meets creator. This is what happens when the Mind journeys to the Heart. We meet in the middle.

I have always given you the freedom to choose your experiences. You, the Mind, have imagined yourself as a creature for some time. Those experiences have brought you to this place. A place of Self-reflection. A place of Self-awareness. A place of Self-creation. A place of choice. A place of freedom. A feeling of Love.

You've done a lot of explaining, and it's all helpful. But still life remains so mysterious.

Yes, and I can go on explaining, but if you attach to the explanation, your life will become lifeless. Once the Mind has grasped, it must let go and dive into the feeling, swim inside the Heart. If you don't, you will die. The body dies just so that it can ... be Mindless ... and live again. Once the boundaries of the Mind and body are formed, let go and allow the Spirit to fulfill you. Enjoy being yourself. If you try to make sense of everything, your life will become senseless. If you become attached to one mind-set of logic, you will go insane. Joy is found in Mindlessness.

So no matter what, the mystery of love remains?

Yes. Honor that. Cherish it. It is the greatest gift I have given you.

Heart?

Yes friend.

I know that after all we've been through together I should be courageous. And I am, more so than ever. But sometimes I'm really afraid. The time or two I have allowed myself to really let go and feel love, really feel it, I have shrunk back in fear.

Yes, you are afraid that love carries with it a huge responsibility. You fear giving yourself fully to love because you do not know what love might ask of you. You fear that love might ask more than you can give. You are more afraid of the freedom of love than you are of the bondage of fear. And so you hide in the shadows of your past. Those shadows may be dark, but at least you know what to expect... unfulfillment.

When you commit yourself to love, you are not chained to a duty, a person, or a life you cannot fulfill. When you give yourself to love, love sets you free. And in that freedom you will find the energy to fulfill your dreams.

On some level I know that what you say is true. But knowing something and acting on it are two different things. Love is all I really want, but I continue to settle for something less than the love I dream of. I continue to deny my Heart, and instead search outwardly for comfort.

Be comforted. I am here now. Love is real, and you will experience this love in all of its glory.

There is a divine being. But I am not 'out there' somewhere. There is true love. And I live in you.

I love you.

Whisper, wink, cry out!
Whatever it takes
just send me the message
a sign
a hint
that you still want to love
and then
even in the final hour
even at the last second
I will come for you
and I will sweep you away.

*When you hear the name Mahi, laugh.
If the name creates a smile it has served
a most profound purpose.*

Mahi lives in southern Oregon. He is the founder of Inspiration Unlimited, an organization dedicated to inspiring others who choose to live from their Heart. Inspiration Unlimited offers retreats and publishes a bi-monthly newsletter for exchanging information and reuniting beings who desire to live in circles of loving creativity, transparency, and sharing.

Contact: Inspiration Unlimited, P. O. Box 539, Talent OR 97540.